Effective strategies to make money as an influencer.

I0409169

HOW TO MONETIZE YOUR PRESENCE ON SOCIAL MEDIA.

KARLO PARKER

CONTENT

ACKNOWLEDGEMENTS

I want to take this opportunity to express my gratitude to all the people who have been instrumental in the creation of this book. First and foremost, I want to thank my current partner, who has been a constant source of support, love, and motivation. Thank you for believing in me and encouraging me every step of the way.

I would also like to thank my father, who has always supported me in everything I do. Your words of encouragement, advice, and presence in my life have been invaluable to me.

To my sisters, thank you for always being there in my life, for your guidance, and for being a source of motivation in challenging times.

Lastly, I want to thank my children, who are my greatest inspiration and motivation in life. Thank you for teaching me the value of patience, perseverance, and unconditional love.

Without the support of these individuals, this book would not have been possible. I am grateful for their presence in my life and for everything they have done for me. Thank you from the bottom of my heart.

INTRODUCTION

In the digital age, social media has become a powerful platform for sharing content, connecting with others, and most importantly, making money! If you have a strong presence on social media and dream of becoming a successful influencer, this book is your ultimate guide. In "The Art of Monetizing Your Presence on Social Media: Effective Strategies to Make Money as an Influencer," you will discover proven strategies and techniques to turn your followers into a consistent source of income.

CHAPTER 1: DISCOVERING YOUR INFLUENCER NICHE

The first step to monetizing your presence on social media is identifying your influencer niche. In what area or theme do you excel? What knowledge or passions can you share with your audience? In this chapter, I will help you define your niche and find your unique voice in the digital world. Additionally, I will provide examples and actionable techniques to help you understand how to apply the concepts presented in the book.

1.1 Identifying Your Influencer Niche

To begin, it's essential to identify the area or theme in which you excel. Make a list of your interests, skills, and passions. Are you good at sports, music, art, science, or any other particular field? Once you have identified your areas of strength, you can determine your influencer niche.

Example: Imagine you are passionate about soccer and have good knowledge about the subject. Your influencer niche could be "soccer for youth," where you would share tips, training techniques, match analysis, and more.

1.2 Researching and Analyzing Niches

Once you have defined your influencer niche, it's important to research and analyze different niches to assess their viability. This involves researching how popular the topic is, who the prominent influencers are in that field, and what type of content is being shared. Here are some techniques to assist you in this process:

> • Explore social media platforms and search for hashtags related to your niche. Analyze the number of followers, engagement on posts, and the quality of content from existing influencers in that field.
>
> • Use tools like Google Trends to understand the demand and interest in your niche over time.
>
> • Research posts and comments from your target audience on blogs, forums, and discussion groups. This will give you an idea of your audience's needs and desires.

Example: Continuing with the "soccer for youth" niche, you could search for hashtags like #youthsoccertraining, #youthsoccertips, and analyze the content and engagement in the posts from existing influencers in those categories.

1.3 Developing a Strategy to Stand Out

Once you have selected your influencer niche, it's time to develop an effective strategy to stand out in that field. Here are some techniques to assist you:

1. Differentiate yourself from other influencers: Identify what makes you unique and how you can stand out in your niche. You can offer a different approach, original content, or a distinctive style.

2. Leverage your strengths: Analyze your skills and knowledge and use them to establish yourself as an authority in your area. For example, if you have experience as a soccer player, you can share your experiences and tips based on your own firsthand knowledge.

3. Identify your target audience: Understand who your ideal followers are, what their needs are, and what type of content would be valuable to them. This will help you create relevant and engaging content for them.

Example: If you want to stand out in the "soccer for youth" niche, you could differentiate yourself by offering practical and accessible content for beginners, providing specific tips for their development in the sport.

1.4 Conducting a Competitive Analysis

In this chapter, you will also discover tools and techniques to conduct a competitive analysis and learn about other influencers in your niche. This will allow you to understand what they are doing well and how you can leverage their successful strategies to drive your own growth.

- Research other influencers in your niche and analyze their content, communication style, promotion strategies, and how they interact with their audience.

- Observe trends on social media related to your niche and adapt your content to keep it fresh and relevant.

- Learn from the mistakes and successes of other influencers and find ways to improve and offer something unique to your audience.

Example: You can follow other influencers in the "soccer for youth" niche, study their posts, see what type of content resonates most with their audience, and find creative ways to address similar topics.

With "Discovering Your Influencer Niche," you will be ready to embark on your path to success as a social media influencer. You will learn how to build a solid foundation and attract a committed and loyal audience, laying the groundwork for effectively monetizing your presence on social media. Remember, the most important thing is to be authentic, offer valuable content, and have a passion for what you do. Good luck on your journey to digital influence!

CHAPTER 2:
BUILDING YOUR
PERSONAL BRAND
ON SOCIAL MEDIA

In this chapter, we will delve into the exciting process of building your personal brand on social media. We will make the information clear and easy to understand. To achieve this, we will expand the chapter, include examples, and viable techniques that help young people understand how they can build their own personal brand on social media.

2.1 Defining Key Elements of Your Personal Brand

We will start by defining the key elements of your personal brand. These elements will help you stand out and connect with your audience. Here are some important aspects to consider:

> • Value proposition: Identify what makes you unique and what value you can offer to your audience. For example, if you are passionate about fashion, your value proposition could be providing style tips and showcasing different outfits to inspire other young people.

> • Tone of voice: Define how you want to communicate with your audience. Do you want to be friendly and approachable, or more formal and educational? The tone of voice should reflect your personality and resonate with your target audience.

> • Visual style: Choose a consistent visual style that represents your personal brand. This includes the design of your posts, the choice of colors, typography, and graphic elements that identify you.

Example: Suppose you are a young person interested in technology and want to build your personal brand in that field. Your value proposition could be sharing reviews and tutorials of technological products to help other young people make informed decisions. Your tone of voice could be friendly and accessible, using a modern visual style and vibrant colors to attract your audience.

2.2 Creating a Mission and Vision Statement

A mission and vision statement will help you establish your goals as an influencer and maintain a clear focus on your content. Here is an example of how you can build your statement:

4.   Mission: Define the primary purpose of your personal brand. For example, "My mission is to help young people discover and enjoy technology in an accessible and fun way."

5.   Vision: Describe how you envision yourself and your brand in the future. For example, "I want to become a trusted reference in the field of technology for young people and be recognized as an influencer who provides valuable and entertaining content."

2.3 Establishing a Consistent Visual Identity

Consistency is key to building a strong personal brand on social media. Here are some techniques to achieve a consistent visual identity:

• Use the same fonts, colors, and styles in all your posts to create a cohesive look.

• Design a logo or choose a distinctive color scheme that represents you and use it across all your platforms.

Example: If you have decided to build your personal brand in the technology field, you can choose bright and vibrant colors that reflect innovation and modernity. Use these colors in your images, videos, and designs. You can also create a simple and recognizable logo that includes elements related to technology.

2.4 Strategies to Increase Your Visibility on Social Media

Once you have established the foundations of your personal brand, it's time to increase your visibility on social media. Here are some key strategies:

- Consistency in content posting: Regularly publish and maintain a consistent presence on your platforms.

- Storytelling: Use personal stories and experiences to emotionally connect with your audience. This will help you create a stronger and lasting connection.

- Optimize your profile on each platform: Ensure you have a clear bio, an attractive profile picture, and links to your other social media accounts.

- Use hashtags effectively: Research popular hashtags in your niche and use them in your posts to expand your reach and reach new followers.

Example: If you are building your personal brand in the technology field, you can use relevant hashtags like #TechForYouth, #TechReviews, or #FavoriteGadgets in your posts to reach an audience interested in that topic.

Building your personal brand on social media is an exciting and challenging process. This chapter has provided you with key tools and knowledge to stand out among other influencers and create an authentic connection with your audience. Remember to be yourself, offer valuable content, and have a passion for what you do. Get ready to open new doors of opportunity and monetize your presence on social media!

CHAPTER 3: CREATING ENGAGING AND QUALITY CONTENT

In this chapter, we will delve into the fascinating world of creating engaging and quality content on social media. We understand that the target audience of this book is minors, so it is essential that the content is clear, understandable, and filled with examples and practical techniques that young people can apply.

3.1 Exploring Content Formats

We will start by exploring the different content formats you can use to capture your audience's attention. Some of these formats include:

> • Written posts: You will learn how to craft clear, concise, and engaging messages that effectively convey your message.
>
> • Images: You will discover how to select and edit eye-catching images that complement your content and generate visual interest.
>
> • Videos: We will explore how to create impactful videos, from script planning to final editing, using accessible tools.
>
> • Live streaming: You will learn how to leverage live streaming to interact in real-time with your audience and create a closer connection.

3.2 Generating Creative Ideas

Idea generation is a crucial step in creating unique and original content. Here are some techniques to help you find inspiration:

6.   Know your audience: Research the interests and needs of your target audience. You can conduct surveys, read comments, or directly interact with them to understand what kind of content they would like to see.

7.   Trend hunting: Stay updated on current trends in your influencer niche and find ways to relate them to your content.

8.   Brainstorming: Dedicate time to generate unrestricted ideas and jot down everything that comes to mind. Then, select the most promising ideas and work on developing them.

Example: If your niche is related to cooking, you could generate content ideas such as healthy breakfast recipes, cake decorating tutorials, or kitchen utensil recommendations.

3.3 Storytelling

Storytelling is a powerful tool to capture attention and emotionally connect with your audience. Here are some tips:

- Structure your content: Use a beginning, middle, and end structure in your posts to maintain your audience's interest.
- Create a compelling hook: Capture the attention of your followers from the start with an intriguing question, an interesting anecdote, or a striking statement.
- Engaging development: Develop your story in a smooth and exciting way, keeping your audience interested and eager to know more.
- Impactful closure: End your story with a clear message, a powerful reflection, or a call to action that motivates your audience to interact with you.

Example: If you are sharing a healthy recipe, you could start by telling a brief personal story about how you discovered the importance of balanced eating and how this particular recipe has helped you stay fit and healthy.

3.4 Quality and Consistency in Content

Quality is essential to maintain your audience's interest and trust. Here are some techniques to improve the quality of your content:

- Editing and design: Learn to use editing tools to enhance the appearance and visual impact of your posts. Pay attention to aspects such as lighting, colors, composition, and text readability.

- Maintain high standards: Do not compromise the quality of your content. It is important to maintain consistency in delivering valuable and relevant content so that your audience remains interested and engaged with you.

Example: If you are sharing a video tutorial, make sure to record it in a well-lit environment, with clear audio and smooth editing. You can also add visual elements like graphics or text to facilitate understanding.

With the creation of engaging and quality content, you will be on the right path to monetize your presence on social media. This chapter has provided practical tools and examples that will allow you to stand out from the crowd and make a lasting impact on your audience. Get ready to captivate your followers with valuable and captivating content.

3.5 Written Posts:

Written posts are a powerful way to communicate with your audience on social media. Through them, you can convey your ideas, knowledge, and emotions in a clear, concise, and engaging manner. Here are some tips for crafting effective messages:

- Clarity: It is crucial that your messages are understandable to your audience. Use simple language and avoid technical terms or complicated jargon. Organize your ideas logically and coherently, ensuring that each paragraph has a clear purpose.

Example: If you are sharing study tips for an exam, you can divide your post into sections such as "Time Management for Studying," "Memorization Techniques," and "Stress Management during Exams."

- Conciseness: On social media, space is limited, so it is important to be concise in your messages. Avoid redundancy and unnecessary words. Be direct and get to the point, conveying your message clearly and without beating around the bush.

Example: Instead of writing "In my personal opinion, I believe that regular exercise is important for maintaining good health," you can simplify it to "Regular exercise is key to good health."

- Engagement: To capture your audience's attention, it is necessary to make your messages engaging. Use descriptive and emotional words that generate interest and curiosity. Include relevant examples or anecdotes that connect with your followers' experiences.

Example: If you are sharing tips for healthy cooking, you can start your post with an intriguing sentence like "Discover how to turn a simple salad into an explosion of flavors and colors that will delight your senses."

Remember to adapt your writing style to the target audience, in this case, minors. Use a friendly and approachable tone, and avoid using complicated technical terms. The key is to effectively and accessibly convey your message so that young people can understand and apply it in their daily lives.

With these techniques, you will be able to write written posts that are engaging, informative, and capable of effectively conveying your message on social media.

3.6 Images:

Images are a powerful tool for capturing the attention of your audience on social media. You will learn how to select and edit attractive images that complement your content and generate visual interest. Here's how to do it:

- Image selection: Choose images that are related to the theme of your content and visually appealing. You can use photographs, illustrations, or graphics that reinforce your message and resonate with your followers.

Example: If you are sharing travel tips, you can select images of stunning tourist destinations, people enjoying travel experiences, or illustrative maps.

- Quality and resolution: Ensure that you use high-quality images with good resolution. Pixelated or blurry images can devalue your content and negatively affect your audience's perception.

- Editing and enhancement: You can use image editing tools to improve their appearance and make them more attractive. Adjust brightness, contrast, saturation, and focus as needed. You can also crop images to focus on key elements.

- Visual consistency: Maintain visual coherence in your images to strengthen your personal brand. Use a consistent visual style, such as a specific color palette or characteristic filter, that aligns with your brand's aesthetics and creates a recognizable visual identity.

Example: If you have a vibrant and colorful aesthetic, you can use images with bright and contrasting tones. If your brand focuses on elegance and simplicity, you can opt for minimalist images with a soft color palette.

Remember to consider copyright when using images. You can search for free image banks or use your own photographs if you have permission.

By selecting and editing attractive images, you can complement your content and generate greater visual interest in your social media posts. This will help capture your audience's attention and effectively convey your message.

3.7 Videos:

Videos are a powerful form of communication on social media. In this chapter, we will explore how to create impactful videos, from script planning to final editing, using accessible tools. Here's how to do it:

- Script planning: Before you start recording, it's important to plan the content of your video. Define the objective and message you want to convey. Organize your ideas into a script that includes an engaging introduction, the development of the topic, and an effective conclusion.

Example: If you are sharing makeup tips, your script can include an introduction that generates intrigue, detailed steps to achieve a specific makeup look, and a closing that motivates your followers to try it.

- Recording: Use a good quality camera, such as your smartphone's camera, to record your videos. Ensure good lighting and clear sound. You can use tripods or stands to keep the camera stable during recording.

- Editing: Use accessible and user-friendly video editing tools to give a professional touch to your recordings. You can trim unnecessary segments, add smooth transitions, insert background music, and enhance the visual and sound quality of your videos.

- Duration and format: Consider the optimal duration for your videos, keeping them short enough to maintain your audience's attention. Also, adapt the video format to different platforms, such as square videos for Instagram or vertical videos for Facebook Stories.

Example: If you are sharing a DIY tutorial on Instagram, you can create a brief and dynamic video that showcases the main steps in a square format, easy to view on a mobile device screen.

Remember to be authentic and show your personality in your videos. This will help establish a stronger connection with your audience.

With script planning, careful recording, and effective editing, you can create impactful videos that attract and captivate your audience on social media. These accessible tools will allow you to effectively convey your messages and make a greater impact.

3.8 Live Streaming:

Live streaming is a powerful tool for interacting with your audience in real-time and creating a closer connection. In this chapter, you will learn how to make the most of live streaming on social media. Here's how to do it:

- Platform selection: Identify the most suitable live streaming platform for your target audience. Some popular options include Instagram Live, Facebook Live, YouTube Live, and Twitch. Consider the features of each platform and the audience you want to reach.

- Topics and content: Plan the topic of your live stream in advance to provide valuable and relevant content to your audience. You can do tutorials, interviews, debates, Q&A sessions, or share behind-the-scenes moments. Keep your live streams interesting and varied to maintain your audience's interest.

Example: If you have a cooking channel, you can do live streams where you prepare recipes in real-time, answer viewers' questions, and share useful tips on culinary techniques.

1.   Real-time interaction: Take advantage of the live nature of the stream to interact directly with your audience. Respond to comments, questions, and greetings from viewers while you are live. Encourage participation and create a sense of community.

2.   Pre-promotion: Announce the date and time of your live stream in advance so that your followers are informed and can join. Use other communication channels such as social media posts, emails, or Instagram Stories to generate anticipation and promote the stream.

During the live stream, remember to maintain a friendly and authentic attitude. Ask questions to your audience, invite them to participate, and share their opinions. This will help create a closer connection and generate a sense of real-time community.

Live streaming is a powerful way to interact with your audience and establish a closer connection. Make use of this opportunity to provide valuable content, interact in real-time, and strengthen your presence on social media.

CHAPTER 4: EXPANDING YOUR AUDIENCE AND BUILDING FOLLOWERS' LOYALTY

In this chapter, we will delve into the exciting world of expanding your audience and building loyalty among your followers on social media. You will learn effective strategies to increase your reach, attract new followers, and techniques to keep your audience engaged and convert them into loyal followers.

Expanding Your Audience:

• Profile Optimization: Make sure your profiles on different social media platforms are complete and well-designed. Use attractive profile pictures and a clear, concise biography that highlights your interests and personality.

Example: If you focus on the fashion world, you can use a profile picture that reflects your unique style and a biography that highlights your main interests in fashion.

9.   Hashtag Research: Research relevant hashtags in your niche and use them strategically in your posts. This will help increase the visibility of your content and attract followers interested in your topic.

Example: If you specialize in fitness, you can use hashtags like #FitnessMotivation, #HealthyLifestyle, or #WorkoutInspiration to reach an audience interested in this subject.

• Collaborations with Other Influencers: Look for opportunities to collaborate with other influencers who have a similar audience to yours. You can do shoutout exchanges, collaborate on content, or even organize joint events to attract the attention of new followers.

Example: If you have a gaming channel, you can collaborate with other popular gamers to do joint streams or create shared videos that benefit both audiences.

Building Followers' Loyalty:

•   Authenticity and Transparency: Be authentic in your interactions with the audience. Show your personality and share your experiences transparently. This will help establish an emotional connection with your followers and build trust.

Example: Share personal anecdotes related to your topic and how they have helped you grow and overcome challenges.

- Responding to Comments and Messages: Take the time to respond to comments and messages from your followers in a timely and personalized manner. This shows that you value their engagement and makes them feel part of an active community.
- Creating a Community: Foster participation from your followers by organizing contests, challenges, or interactive activities. This creates a sense of belonging and commitment in your community.

Example: Organize a drawing contest where your followers can submit their creations related to your topic and offer a prize to the winner.

In this chapter, I will teach you effective strategies to increase your reach on social media, attract new followers, and techniques to keep your audience engaged and convert them into loyal followers. These strategies will help you expand your influence and establish a solid base of followers on social platforms.

Increasing Your Reach and Attracting New Followers:

- Relevant and Valuable Content: To attract new followers, it is essential to offer relevant and valuable content. Understand your target audience and create content that meets their needs and interests. Research current trends and market demands to generate fresh and engaging ideas.

Example: If you cater to a teenage audience interested in fashion, you can create style tutorial videos, affordable shopping recommendations, or tips on outfit combinations.

- Social Media Advertising: Utilize paid promotion strategies to reach a wider audience. Social media platforms offer powerful advertising tools that allow you to segment and target your ads to a specific demographic group. Take advantage of these tools to increase the visibility of your profile and attract new followers.

Example: Set up Instagram ads that target people interested in your topic and within the age range of your target audience.

- Strategic Collaborations: Establish collaborations with other influencers or brands that share similar values and audiences. By partnering with them, you can leverage their reach and visibility to attract new followers. You can do shoutout exchanges, collaborate on content, or even organize joint events.

Example: If you are a travel blogger, you can collaborate with a luggage brand to create joint content or engage in cross-promotion on social media.

Keeping Your Audience Engaged and Converting Them into Loyal Followers:

- Active Interaction: Maintain active interaction with your audience. Respond to comments on your posts, thank followers for their support, and engage in conversations related to your topic. This shows that you value your followers and fosters a closer relationship.

- Varied and Regular Content: Offer diverse content to keep your audience interested. Combine different formats such as images, videos, written posts, polls, questions, and live streams. Additionally, maintain a regular posting frequency so that your followers stay engaged and return to your profile for fresh content.

- Exclusivity and Benefits: Offer exclusive benefits to your loyal followers. This can include early access to content, discounts on products or services, participation in special giveaways, or memberships with additional perks. These incentives reinforce a sense of belonging and loyalty toward your brand.

Example: If you have a cooking YouTube channel, you can offer exclusive recipes or free cookbook downloads to your subscribed followers.

By implementing these strategies and techniques, you will be able to increase your reach, attract new followers, and maintain long-lasting engagement with your audience. Remember that consistency, authenticity, and delivering value are crucial in turning followers into loyal supporters.

Get ready to build a strong community on social media and effectively monetize your presence!

CHAPTER 5: COLLABORATIONS AND BRAND SPONSORSHIPS: GENERATING REVENUE THROUGH STRATEGIC PARTNERSHIPS

In this chapter, we will delve into the exciting world of collaborations and brand sponsorships on social media. We will learn how to leverage our influence and presence on social networks to establish strategic partnerships with relevant brands and generate additional income.

Selecting the Right Brands to Collaborate With:

We will start by understanding the importance of selecting the right brands to collaborate with. It is essential that brands align with your niche and values and have a strong reputation and credibility. I will guide you through the process of identifying brands that resonate with your audience and interest you in order to establish strong and beneficial relationships.

Example: If your content focuses on wellness and a healthy lifestyle, you could seek collaborations with organic food brands, sports brands, or eco-friendly product companies.

Introducing Yourself to Brands and Negotiating Agreements:

You will learn how to present yourself to brands in a professional and convincing manner, highlighting your value as an influencer. We will also explore different types of collaborations, from sponsored posts to product promotions and events. I will teach you how to communicate clearly and establish mutual expectations to ensure a successful collaboration.

Example: When contacting a brand for a collaboration, you could emphasize your achievements and experience in the specific area and propose creative ideas on how you could uniquely and attractively promote their products or services.

We will also delve into the different types of collaborations you can undertake with brands on social media. These include, but are not limited to, sponsored posts and product and event promotions. I will provide you with examples and techniques for each type of collaboration, so you can understand how they work and how to make the most of them.

> • Sponsored posts: You will learn how to create sponsored posts that are effective and authentic. I will show you how to seamlessly integrate the brand's product or service into your content in a

way that is interesting and relevant to your audience. Additionally, I will teach you how to clearly and transparently communicate that it is a sponsored collaboration, maintaining the trust of your followers.

Example: If you are collaborating with a clothing brand, you could create a post showcasing how to mix and match different pieces from their collection into different outfits. You can highlight the benefits of each item and how they suit different occasions.

10. Product promotions: We will explore how to carry out product promotions through reviews, demonstrations, or recommendations. I will teach you how to present products in an appealing and persuasive manner, highlighting their features and benefits. Additionally, you will learn how to set clear expectations with the brand regarding the duration and frequency of the promotions.

Example: If you are promoting a beauty product, you could create a video demonstration showing how to apply it and the results that can be achieved. You can share your personal experience with the product and highlight the aspects you like the most.

• Event promotions: You will discover how to collaborate with brands in promoting events such as product launches, themed parties, or special activities. I will show you how to generate anticipation and excitement among your audience using anticipation techniques and creating content related to the event. Additionally, you will learn how to coordinate collaboration details with the brand, such as information dissemination, participation in the event, and post-event coverage.

Example: If you are collaborating in promoting a concert, you could publish pre-event content such as interviews with the artists or reviews of their previous albums. During the concert, you could livestream from the venue and share highlights with your followers.

Clear communication and setting mutual expectations are crucial in ensuring a successful collaboration. I will provide you with guidelines and techniques for establishing effective communication with the brand, from the initial introduction to negotiating the details of the agreement. You will learn how to express your ideas convincingly and consider the goals and requirements of the brand to achieve a harmon.

Remember that the success of collaborations depends on the authenticity and trust you maintain with your audience. You must always ensure that the products or services you promote align with the values and interests of your audience and provide real value. This way, you can maintain the loyalty and engagement of your followers and effectively generate additional income as a social media influencer.

Authenticity in Brand Collaborations:

We will discuss the importance of authenticity when collaborating with brands. You will learn how to maintain your integrity and the trust of your audience when promoting products or services. You will discover strategies to organically and cohesively integrate collaborations into your content so that they feel authentic and valuable to your audience.

Example: If you're promoting a product, you can share your genuine personal experience with it and highlight how it has genuinely improved your life. Avoid excessive promotion and focus on conveying the real benefits the product can offer. Another important aspect is consistency in your collaborations. Learn how to select brands and products that genuinely interest you and align with your style and theme. Maintaining consistency in your collaborations will help your audience perceive your content as authentic and cohesive. You'll avoid promoting products or services that don't fit your profile and could generate skepticism among your followers.

Remember that authenticity is key to maintaining a strong relationship with your audience and ensuring long-term success as an influencer. By focusing on authentic and valuable collaborations, you'll make a positive impact on your community and strengthen the trust relationship with your followers.

There are several techniques you can use to organically and cohesively integrate collaborations into your content, ensuring they are authentic and valuable to your audience. Here are some of them:

- Careful brand selection: It's crucial to choose brands that align with your values and are relevant to your audience. Research and thoroughly get to know the brands you want to collaborate with, ensuring that their products or services are genuinely useful and beneficial to your community.

- Personal experience: To authentically promote, it's important to have tried and experienced the products or services of the brands you collaborate with. By having personal experience, you can speak confidently about the benefits and features, offering recommendations based on your own experiences.

- Contextualization in your content: Integrate collaborations naturally into the context of your content. Avoid promotions that feel isolated or out of place. For example, if you're a fitness influencer, you can show how you use a particular product during your exercise routines or share healthy recipes using ingredients from a specific brand.

- Storytelling: Use the power of storytelling to provide

context to your collaborations. Share how the product or service has had a positive impact on your life or the life of someone close to you. By emotionally connecting with your audience through authentic stories, you'll generate greater interest and credibility.

- Transparency and honesty: It's essential to be transparent with your audience when doing collaborations. Clearly indicate when it's a sponsored collaboration to maintain the trust of your followers. Additionally, provide honest and balanced opinions about the products or services, highlighting both their positive aspects and potential limitations.
- Visual and aesthetic integration: Ensure that collaborations visually integrate into your content. Use high-quality photographs or videos that showcase the products or services in an appealing and consistent manner with your aesthetic style. Visual consistency will contribute to promotions feeling organic and an integral part of your content.

Remember that these techniques should be applied consistently and always considering the interests and needs of your audience. By using strategies that respect authenticity and provide value to your community, you'll build strong relationships with brands and maintain the support of your followers in the long run.

Compensation and Negotiation:

We will explore the topic of compensation and negotiation in brand collaborations. You will learn how to establish fair pricing for your collaborations and structure agreements that provide long-term economic benefits. I will provide practical tips for setting rates and ensuring you receive appropriate compensation for your work and influence.

Example: When negotiating an agreement, consider factors such as the reach of your audience, the duration and level of required involvement, and the value you bring to the brand. Maintain open communication and seek a balance that is beneficial for both you and the brand.

Within the realm of brand collaborations, it's crucial to understand the topic of compensation and negotiation. You will learn how to establish fair pricing for your collaborations and structure agreements that provide long-term economic benefits. Here are practical tips to set rates and ensure you receive appropriate compensation for your work and influence.

- Know the value of your influence: Before negotiating any collaboration agreement, it's important to have a clear idea of the value you bring as an influencer. Evaluate your reach, audience interaction, specific niche, and other relevant factors. This will allow you to establish fair and well-founded prices based on your real influence.
- Research industry standards: Investigate the prices and rates typically used in the influencer marketing industry. Familiarize yourself with the compensation ranges for similar collaborations to the ones you seek to establish. This will give you a solid foundation for negotiation and ensure you receive compensation aligned with your influence and the reach of your audience.
- Consider your time and resource investment: In addition to your influence, consider the time and resources you will invest in the collaboration. If it requires extra effort, such as creating specific content or participating in events, it's fair to receive compensation that reflects this additional dedication.
- Establish collaboration packages: Instead of only offering individual sponsored posts, consider offering

collaboration packages that include multiple posts or promotional activities. This can generate long-term economic benefits and strengthen the relationship with the brand.

- Negotiate with clarity and confidence: When negotiating, communicate your rates and expectations clearly and confidently. Don't be afraid to express the value you bring and the benefits the brand will gain by collaborating with you. Maintain a professional attitude and be open to negotiation, but also ensure you receive fair compensation for your work.

- Consider long-term agreements: If you have a strong relationship with a brand and both parties are satisfied with the collaboration, consider establishing long-term agreements. These agreements can provide you with economic stability and mutual benefits in the long run.

Remember that each collaboration is unique and may require a personalized approach to negotiation. Always maintain clear communication, set mutual expectations, and ensure the agreement is beneficial for both you and the brand.

With "Brand Collaborations and Sponsorships," you'll be prepared to leverage monetization opportunities through strategic partnerships. You'll learn how to build strong relationships with relevant brands, authentically promote products or services, and generate additional income as a social media influencer.

CHAPTER 6: GENERATING INCOME THROUGH ADVERTISING ON SOCIAL MEDIA

In this chapter, we will dive into the fascinating world of generating income through advertising on social media. You will discover effective strategies to leverage your presence on digital platforms and monetize it by inserting advertisements.

We will start by understanding the different types of advertising on social media. We will explore the available options such as native ads, video ads, story ads, and sponsored ads. These are some examples of how brands can promote themselves on social media to reach their audience. You will learn how these types of advertising work and how you can effectively integrate them into your content.

For example, native ads are those that adapt to the format and style of the platform they are displayed on. They may look like regular posts but contain promotional information. Video ads, on the other hand, are short clips that capture the audience's attention and allow them to learn more about a product or service. Story ads are images or videos that play automatically between users' stories, while sponsored ads are paid posts that appear in users' feeds.

Here are some effective strategies to leverage your presence on digital platforms and monetize it through the insertion of advertising:

• Identify your target audience: Before starting to insert ads in your content, it's important to understand who you are targeting. Identify the interests, needs, and demographic characteristics of your audience to offer them relevant ads.

• Create quality content: Quality and engaging content is crucial to maintain the interest of your audience. Make sure to produce valuable and entertaining content that generates an emotional connection with your followers. This will increase the effectiveness of the ads you insert.

- Select relevant ads: Choose ads that are related to your niche and relevant to your audience. This will ensure that the ads are organically integrated into your content and perceived as valuable by your followers.

- Opt for appropriate advertising formats: Explore different ad formats such as native ads, video ads, or story ads, and choose those that best fit your content and your audience's preferences.

- Experiment with strategic placements: Try different placements within your content to insert the ads. Observe which locations generate better results in terms of click-through rates (CTR) and ad performance.

- Use effective calls to action (CTA): Include clear and persuasive calls to action in your ads to motivate your audience to interact with them. Well-designed CTAs can increase engagement rates and, therefore, your advertising revenue.

- Monitor and analyze results: Pay attention to metrics and data related to your ads, such as CTR, impressions, and generated revenue. Use this information to optimize your strategies and make informed decisions on how to improve your advertising performance.

Remember that authenticity and quality of your content are crucial. Avoid overcrowding your content with too many ads, as this can be annoying to your audience and harm your credibility. Find a suitable balance so that ads are seamlessly and valuable integrated into your content.

Next, we will discuss the process of establishing partnerships with online advertising platforms. For example, you can register for monetization programs like Google AdSense or participate in affiliate programs of relevant brands in your niche.

Utilize these platforms to optimize your ad spaces and maximize your income. It's important to consider the policies and guidelines of the advertising platforms to ensure that you comply with the rules and avoid any issues. Each platform has its own policies, such as the number and placement of allowed ads. By following these rules, you can maximize your earnings and maintain a positive relationship with the advertising platforms.

We will also explore strategies to increase your advertising revenue. One effective technique is to improve your click-through rates (CTR) by optimizing your ads and calls to action. You can use attractive visuals, persuasive messages, and eye-catching buttons to encourage your audience to click on the ads. You will learn to analyze and utilize data and metrics to evaluate the performance of your ads and make informed decisions to optimize your earnings.

Lastly, we will emphasize the importance of maintaining a balance between advertising and organic content. It's essential for your followers to feel that the ads you display are relevant and valuable to them. Find the appropriate balance to meet your audience's needs and generate income without compromising the quality and authenticity of your content. For example, you can intersperse ads between regular posts or use creative captions and descriptions to make the ads feel less intrusive. You can also employ targeting techniques to show relevant ads to specific segments of your audience.

With this information, you will be prepared to seize the monetization opportunities through advertising on social media. Strategically utilize ad spaces, optimize your earnings, and maintain a balance between advertising and organic content.

CHAPTER 7: EXPANDING YOUR INCOME OPPORTUNITIES

In this chapter, we will explore the importance of expanding your income sources as a social media influencer. You will learn effective strategies to diversify your income opportunities and reduce dependence on a single source.

We will start by exploring different business models you can implement. For example, you may consider creating and selling digital products. These can include ebooks, online courses, or exclusive memberships that provide added value to your audience. You will learn how to identify the needs of your target audience and develop products that meet those needs effectively.

Identify the specific needs and desires of your target audience. This will allow you to develop digital products that effectively meet those needs.

For example, if your audience is interested in learning about a particular topic, you could create an online course that addresses that topic in a detailed and practical manner. This way, you'll be providing real and useful value to your followers.

Utilize various techniques to design and present your digital products attractively. Use online tools and platforms to create visually appealing ebooks and interactive courses. Explore strategies to promote and sell your digital products, such as using effective marketing campaigns and implementing launch strategies.

Another option to diversify your income sources is to offer additional services to your audience. Using your knowledge and skills, you could offer consulting services, mentorship, or personalized guidance. This will allow you to provide more direct support to your followers and generate additional income through your specialized services.

By exploring different business models and developing digital products that meet your audience's needs, you'll be able to effectively diversify your income sources.

Identify your opportunities in the market, create high-quality products, and promote them strategically. Prepare to expand your income opportunities and ensure financial stability as a social media influencer.

Consider the possibility of offering additional services. Using your skills and knowledge, you could offer consulting services, mentorship, or personalized collaborations with your followers.

I'll provide guidance on how to establish appropriate fees and structure your services to maximize your earnings.

Also, consider monetization through affiliate marketing. Learn how to establish strategic partnerships with brands relevant to your audience and effectively promote products or services. Discover how to generate income through commissions for every sale made through your recommendations. I'll teach you techniques to create persuasive and authentic content that motivates your followers to make purchases.

Additionally, explore the possibility of earning income through online events. You can organize webinars, virtual conferences, or online workshops and monetize audience participation through ticket sales or sponsorships. Learn strategies to promote and highlight the value proposition of your events, attracting an interested audience and generating additional income.

Prepare to maximize your earnings and ensure your financial stability as a social media influencer.

Here are some guidelines and tips you can follow:

> • Research the market: Before setting your fees, it's important to research the market and understand the average rates in your industry and specific niche. Look at what other influencers with a similar profile to yours are charging for similar services. This will give you an idea of how your work is valued and help you

establish competitive rates.

• Evaluate your experience and value: Consider your experience, skills, and the quality of your services when setting your fees. If you have a distinguished track record, unique skills, or high-quality content, you can justify higher rates. Remember that your rates should reflect the value you bring to your clients or collaborators.

• Determine your costs and profit goals: Before setting your fees, it's essential to take into account your operational costs and profit goals. This includes expenses such as equipment, software, marketing tools, taxes, and other costs related to your influencer activity. Make sure to cover these costs and establish a reasonable profit margin.

• Offer package options: Instead of having only a fixed rate, consider offering different package options to meet the needs and budgets of your clients. You can create basic, intermediate, and premium packages that include different levels of service and prices. This will allow you to attract a variety of clients and increase your income generation opportunities.

• Consider demand and competition: The demand for your services and the level of competition in your niche can also influence your fees. If there is high demand for your services or if you are one of the few influencers specialized in a specific area, you may consider raising your rates. On the other hand, if the competition is fierce and you need to stand out, you could offer more competitive rates to attract clients.

• Adjust your fees over time: Remember that your rates don't have to be fixed forever. As you gain more experience, grow in your niche, and the demand for your services increases, you can gradually adjust your fees. Conduct regular reviews and assess whether your rates remain suitable in relation to the value you offer and the overall market.

In addition to setting appropriate fees, it's important to structure your services effectively to maximize your earnings. This involves clearly defining what each service includes, setting limits and terms, and transparently communicating them to your clients. You can also consider offering additional or complementary services that can generate additional income, such as personalized consultations, paid courses, or exclusive collaborations.

Remember that finding the right balance between the value you offer, your fees, and customer satisfaction is crucial for long-term success. Stay open to adjusting your strategies as you grow as an influencer and gain more experience in the market.

CHAPTER 8: FINANCIAL MANAGEMENT AND LONG-TERM PLANNING

In this final chapter, we will delve into the fascinating world of financial management and long-term planning, two key elements to ensure your success as a social media influencer. We will learn practical strategies and concrete examples that will help you manage your income, establish clear financial goals, and ensure your long-term economic stability.

We will start by understanding the importance of financial organization and how to keep detailed records of your income and expenses. This practice will allow you to have a clear view of your financial situation and make informed decisions.

I will teach you how to establish a realistic budget and use financial management tools and software that will simplify this process.

A budget will help you have a clear picture of your finances, allowing you to make informed decisions about how to use your money. You will learn to identify your sources of income, whether through collaborations, social media advertising, or other opportunities related to your influence. Additionally, you will understand how to classify your expenses into categories such as food, transportation, entertainment, among others.

Using financial management tools and software will provide you with greater efficiency in the budgeting process. These tools will allow you to automatically record and monitor your income and expenses, saving you time and providing you with a clearer view of your financial situation.

There are various options for software and mobile applications that can assist you in this process. Some of them offer features such as automatic categorization of expenses, tracking financial goals, generating reports and graphs, and synchronizing with your bank accounts and credit cards. By using these tools and techniques, you will be able to establish a realistic budget and maintain constant control over your finances. This will enable you to make informed decisions, adjust your expenses as needed, and maintain a healthy long-term financial management.

Remember that the main goal of establishing a budget is to ensure effective management of your resources and guarantee your financial stability. Through examples and practical advice, you will learn how to create a budget that suits your needs and helps you achieve your financial goals.

Next, we will explore savings and investment techniques that will help you build a solid foundation for your financial future. You will learn how to establish an emergency fund, which will provide you with peace of mind and security in case of unexpected events. Additionally, I will guide you through the world of investments, introducing you to different options and teaching you how to diversify your assets to maximize your long-term growth opportunities and financial protection.

When it comes to savings and investment techniques, there are various strategies you can use to ensure your long-term financial stability. Here are some techniques and examples you may consider:

Establish an emergency fund: It is recommended to allocate a portion of your income to an emergency fund that helps you cope with unexpected situations. It is generally suggested to save at least 3 to 6 months' worth of basic expenses in this fund. For example, if your monthly expenses average $500, your goal would be to save between $1,500 and $3,000 in your emergency fund.

Automatic savings: Setting up an automatic savings system is an excellent way to ensure that you regularly allocate a portion of your income to savings. You can establish an automatic transfer from one account to another, assigning a specific percentage of your income to your savings account. This way, you won't have to worry about saving manually, and the process will be easier and more consistent.

Diversify your investments: An important technique is to diversify your investments to reduce risk and maximize long-term earning potential. You can consider investing in different assets, such as stocks, bonds, mutual funds, or real estate. By diversifying, you will be spreading your money across different areas, allowing you to take advantage of opportunities and mitigate potential losses.

Retirement Planning: Although it may seem distant, it is essential to start planning and saving for your retirement from an early age. You can consider options such as individual retirement accounts (IRAs), employer-sponsored pension plans, or long-term investment funds. Setting specific goals and allocating a portion of your income to retirement savings will help ensure financial security in the future.

Investments in Education: If you are underage, investing in your education is one of the best financial decisions you can make. Obtaining a good education will provide you with professional growth opportunities and better long-term economic prospects. You can consider saving for future education expenses, such as college tuition, specialized courses, or training programs.

Remember that each person has unique financial circumstances and goals, so it is important to adapt these techniques to your particular situation. Consulting with a financial advisor can be very helpful in receiving personalized guidance and making informed decisions about your savings and investments.

Tax Planning: Key aspects of taxes and tax obligations to consider as a social media influencer.

When discussing tax planning for social media influencers, it is important to consider key aspects of taxes and tax obligations. Below, I will provide you with some examples and techniques you could consider:

• Income Tracking and Reporting: As an influencer, it is crucial to keep detailed records of your income from collaborations, advertising, or any other source. Make sure to maintain accurate records of your earnings and declare all your income in your tax return.

• Identification of Tax Deductions: As a taxpayer, you have the right to claim certain tax deductions allowed by law. Identifying and utilizing these deductions can help reduce your tax burden. Some common deductions for influencers may include expenses related to equipment and tools necessary for your work, hired professional services, advertising expenses, travel costs, and accommodation for events related to your influencer activity, among others. It is important to keep all relevant records and receipts to support your deductions.

• Establishing an Appropriate Legal Structure: Depending on your circumstances and income level, it may be beneficial to establish a legal structure for your influencer activity. This could include creating a sole proprietorship or establishing a legal entity such as an LLC (limited liability company). Consult with a legal advisor or a tax specialist to determine the most suitable structure for your needs and goals.

• Quarterly Tax Payments: As an influencer, you may need to make estimated quarterly tax payments if your income is not subject to regular tax withholdings. These quarterly payments help ensure that you meet your tax obligations in a timely manner and avoid penalties or sanctions. Consult with an accountant or tax advisor to determine if you need to make quarterly payments and calculate the appropriate amount to pay.

• Stay Updated with Tax Legislation: Tax laws can change, and it is essential to stay updated with any changes that may affect your situation as an influencer. Read and stay informed about relevant tax regulations and legislation for your country or region. Additionally, consider seeking advice from a tax professional who can provide you with up-to-date and accurate guidance.

Remember that tax obligations may vary depending on the jurisdiction and local tax laws. Therefore, it is important to consult with a tax advisor or a tax specialist to obtain specific guidance regarding your individual situation.

We will discuss the importance of establishing clear financial goals and how to create an action plan to achieve them. Having well-defined financial goals is essential for directing your efforts and making sound financial decisions. Below, I will show you how you can do it:

• Define Specific Financial Goals: Start by identifying your short, medium, and long-term financial objectives. These goals could include saving to purchase a desired item, paying off debts, creating an emergency fund, investing for retirement, or acquiring a home. Ensure that your goals are clear, realistic, and quantifiable.

• Prioritize Your Goals: Order your financial goals based on their importance and the timeframe in which you want to achieve them. This will help you focus your resources and efforts on the most relevant goals for you. You may need to make sacrifices or adjust your expenses to prioritize certain financial goals.

• Set Deadlines and Break Down Your Goals: Define realistic deadlines for each financial goal. Then, break down your goals into smaller, achievable steps. For example, if your goal is to save a certain amount of money within a year, set monthly or quarterly milestones to monitor your progress and make adjustments if necessary.

• Create an Action Plan: Develop a detailed plan that guides you toward achieving your financial goals. Identify specific actions you need to take, such as reducing expenses, increasing your income, investing in certain assets, or acquiring additional skills. Assign deadlines to each action and regularly track your progress.

• Review and Adjust Your Plan: As you progress toward your financial goals, it is important to review and adjust your action plan as needed. Evaluate your progress periodically and make adjustments if circumstances change or if you encounter unexpected obstacles. Maintain flexibility to adapt to new opportunities or challenges that may arise.

Remember that achieving financial goals requires discipline, commitment, and perseverance. Keep your focus on your objectives, celebrate your achievements along the way, and maintain the motivation to keep moving forward. With a solid action plan and the right determination, you can reach your financial goals and secure a better long-term economic situation.

Prepare to ensure your financial well-being and enjoy the rewards of your work as a social media influencer.

ABOUT THE AUTHOR

Karlo Parker is a successful entrepreneur who has dedicated his time and effort to creating online stores for others. With extensive experience in e-commerce and a clear vision of market trends and opportunities, Karlo has helped many people make the leap into the world of online commerce.

Since his first e-commerce project, Karlo has been devoted to helping individuals create online stores that are attractive, functional, and profitable. With a passion for design and technology, Karlo has built online stores for a wide variety of products and market niches, and has helped his clients expand their businesses and achieve their sales goals.

In addition to his e-commerce expertise, Karlo is known for his focus on customer service and customer satisfaction. He is always willing to listen to the needs and desires of his clients and works closely with them to ensure that their online stores meet their expectations.

www.ingramcontent.com/pod-product-compliance
Lightning Source LLC
Chambersburg PA
CBHW062259290526
45794CB00006B/2622